# END TIMES IN REAL TIME OFFICIAL WORKBOOK

## DISCERN THE SIGNS OF THE TIMES AND ANNIHILATE THE ANTI-CHRIST AGENDA

JON HAMILL

JOLENE HAMILL

DESTINY IMAGE

Destiny Image P.O. Box 310, Shippensburg, PA 17257-0310

This book and all other Destiny Image's books are available at Christian bookstores and distributors worldwide.

For Worldwide Distribution.

Reach us on the Internet: www.destinyimage.com.

ISBN 13 TP: 9798881504625

ISBN 13 eBook: 9798881504632

# CONTENTS

# INTRODUCTION

Welcome to "End Times in Real Time: Official Workbook," a comprehensive guide designed to navigate the profound realities of our era through the lens of biblical prophecy and personal spiritual growth. This workbook is your companion to understanding and engaging with the turbulent yet transformative times prophesied in Scripture and unfolding in our world today.

## UNPACKING THE PROPHETIC ERA

We are living in extraordinary times—a period where the signs of the End Times, as outlined in biblical texts, are manifesting with increasing clarity and intensity. From geopolitical shifts and cultural upheavals to spiritual awakenings and significant moral challenges, the world seems to be on the precipice of major changes. These are not just random occurrences but are, in many respects, fulfillments of prophecies laid down thousands of years ago.

KEY TAKEAWAYS

1. **Understanding the Times**: This workbook is structured to help you discern the times through a biblical perspective. It equips you to recognize the signs of the End Times not with fear, but with the wisdom and understanding that God provides to those who seek Him. Through scriptural study and guided reflections, you'll learn to see the world events not just as news but as a narrative being woven by God's sovereign hand.

2. **Personal Spiritual Preparedness**: More than ever, these times call for personal spiritual readiness. This workbook provides practical steps to ensure that your relationship with God is robust and that you are spiritually equipped to face whatever challenges may come. Through prayers, reflective questions, and actionable steps, you'll be invited to deepen your faith, enhance your spiritual disciplines, and cultivate a life of righteousness and holiness.

3. **Engaging with Prophetic Insight**: The workbook draws on contemporary prophetic voices alongside biblical prophecy to offer a rounded understanding of what the scriptures say about the last days. By integrating insights from respected prophetic leaders with deep dives into biblical texts, you are encouraged to actively engage with God's revelations for our time.

4. **Community and Collaboration**: In these times, the role of the Christian community becomes even more critical. This workbook encourages forming and

fostering godly relationships that strengthen your faith and provide mutual support. Activities and discussions designed for group settings will help you and your peers sharpen each other as "iron sharpens iron" (Proverbs 27:17).

5. **Practical Application of Biblical Principles**: Each chapter of the workbook translates biblical principles into actionable steps that you can apply in your daily life. Whether it's navigating personal trials, participating in community and church life, or engaging with societal issues, the workbook provides guidance on living out your faith in practical, impactful ways.

## WHAT TO EXPECT

As you journey through this workbook, expect to be challenged, encouraged, and transformed. Each section is designed to not only provide knowledge but also to spur you into action. The structure of the workbook—comprising detailed summaries, reflective questions, and actionable steps—aims to facilitate both understanding and practical application.

- **Cultivating a Resilient Faith**: Learn to stand firm in your beliefs even as the world around you shifts. This workbook will help you build a faith that not only endures but also thrives in adversity.

- **Equipping for Spiritual Battles**: Gain insights into the armor of God (Ephesians 6:10-18) and how to wield spiritual weapons effectively, ensuring you are well-prepared for the spiritual warfare that intensifies in the End Times.

- **Engaging in Redemptive Action:** Be inspired to act on your faith in ways that bring light and salt to the world (Matthew 5:13-16). This workbook encourages a life of active faith that engages with the world to bring about spiritual and societal transformation.

# CHAPTER 1

# A RELENTLESS VIGIL

**Be strong and courageous; do not be afraid nor dismayed, for the Lord your God is with you wherever you go. (Joshua 1:9 NKJV)**

In "A Relentless Vigil," I invite you into a world that feels eerily reminiscent of biblical prophecies coming to life. Reflecting on the infectious chorus of REM's hit from the eighties, "IT'S THE END OF THE WORLD AS WE KNOW IT," I draw a parallel between the seemingly innocent times of my youth and the complex era we navigate today—an era marked by **End Times Awareness**. This awareness isn't just about recognizing signs but understanding our current geopolitical and social climate as a reflection of these prophetic times.

During my days as a young journalism student, transformed by a radical encounter with Jesus in college, I experienced first-hand the **Transformation Through Crisis**. My journey from a Unitarian background to a committed Christian was met with misunderstanding and alienation from family and friends. This personal transformation mirrored the larger call to adapt and thrive spiritually in tumultuous times, emphasizing the need for personal resilience and spiritual depth.

Now, residing and ministering in the heart of Washington D.C., I am granted a unique perspective on the unfolding of global events. **Living and Ministering in Washington D.C.** offers not only a front-row seat to political maneuvers but also a daily reminder of the prophetic significance of our times. Here, discussions in the corridors of power often echo biblical themes, bringing the realities of the **End Times as Current Reality** into sharper focus. It's from this vantage point that I speak to you, urging a readiness and vigilance that transcends mere survival.

In this book, I am committed not to rehearsing well-trod theories of escape but rather to **Spiritual Equipage for the End Times.** We will explore not just how to survive but to shine and overcome amidst these challenges. Understanding God's purposes during these times is essential, which is why we delve into the significance of **Covenant and Idolatry**. Our covenant with Christ is the bedrock of our faith, setting us apart and empowering us to confront and reject the idolatries that so often ensnare us.

Reflecting on historical patterns, it's clear that every generation faces its form of antichrist spirit. This recurring challenge underscores the **Role of Personal and Collective History** in shaping our responses to spiritual and societal crises. We are called not just to anticipate an escape but to actively engage in the spiritual battles of our day.

One of the most profound experiences that shaped my understanding of the end times involved a personal visitation from Jesus. In this encounter, I understood Jesus as the **Jesus as the Bridegroom**, longing for His bride—the Church—to return to Him fully. This personal revelation was transformative, emphasizing that our struggles and watchfulness mirror Jesus' own vigil for His beloved.

As we journey through this book, we'll uncover **Practical and Spiritual Strategies** that move beyond abstract eschatology to tangible, actionable faith. These strategies are designed to equip you with the knowledge and tools to navigate these times not with fear but with authority and effectiveness.

Ultimately, the goal is to empower you to **Empowerment to Prevail** over the antichrist forces in your own life and community. This empowerment starts with a deep, personal overcoming and extends to influencing the world around you in significant, God-honoring ways.

Join me in this exploration and be equipped not just to face the end times but to engage them as a proactive, empowered, and spiritually vibrant believer. Together, let's forge a path through these challenging times, grounded in the truth of Scripture and activated by a faith that transforms.

**REFLECTIVE QUESTIONS**

1. How does the concept of the end times influence your daily life and spiritual practice?
2. Reflect on a personal crisis that transformed your spiritual life. How did that experience draw you closer to or further from God?
3. In what ways can living in a politically and socially dynamic environment like Washington D.C. affect one's spiritual perception and actions?
4. How do you understand the concept of covenant in your personal spiritual journey? Are there idols or practices that challenge your commitment to this covenant?
5. What practical steps can you take to actively engage

with the challenges and opportunities presented by the end times?

## Actionable Steps

- **Cultivate** a Deeper Understanding: Invest time in studying biblical prophecies and contemporary interpretations to deepen your understanding of the times we live in.
- **Equip** Yourself with Spiritual Tools: Engage in prayer, fasting, and communal worship to build spiritual resilience and readiness.
- **Engage** Others in Conversation: Start discussions within your community about the relevance of end times teachings and how they can be practically applied to uplift and prepare one another.

## Journaling Prompt

Reflect on the current events in your life and in the world around you. How do you see these as part of the 'end times' narrative? What is God speaking to you through these circumstances? Write about how you can align more closely with God's purposes during these times.

# TWO BURNING LAMPS

**Be strong and courageous; do not be afraid nor dismayed, for the Lord your God is with you wherever you go. (Joshua 1:9 NKJV)**

In "Two Burning Lamps," the echo of history reminds us that sometimes the most significant calls to action are the ones we initially overlook, much like missing our wallet in plain sight or misplacing our phone only to discover it's been in our pocket all along. This realization struck my wife Jolene and me profoundly as we delved into our spiritual calling during these end times. Initially, the **end times** were a distant, almost forgotten aspect of our faith. However, when the prophetic alarm sounded, it shocked us into recognition, revealing that this calling was always part of our destiny.

Reflecting on the 250th anniversary of Paul Revere's legendary midnight ride that ignited the American Revolution, I find a compelling parallel in our current spiritual journey. Just as Revere's ride was a pivotal moment of awakening for the American colonies, so too is our **prophetic calling** meant to awaken a generation to the imminence of Christ's return. The prophecy given to me by Cindy Jacobs in 2000, which at first seemed to align more with revival, was actually a clarion call preparing us to be modern-day forerunners, echoing Revere's message of imminent arrival. But instead of warning of the British, we are to announce the coming of the Lord.

This **prophetic warning** to be a voice in the wilderness, much like John the Baptist, became clear only with time. Initially, it was easy to interpret Cindy's prophecy as pertaining solely to spiritual revival—after all, the signs of the times seemed distant and our immediate focus was on awakening hearts to God's presence. Yet, as events unfolded—especially through the crises of 2020—it became evident that these were not just harbingers of revival but were directly tied to the **midnight crises** of end-time events. The pandemic, societal upheavals, and the stark political divisions exposed the fabric of our society and the urgency of our mission.

The call to be **two burning lamps** in the darkness of our times is not just metaphorical. It is a literal summoning to ignite and carry the fire of God's presence and power wherever we go, much like the lamps that guided Paul Revere on his midnight ride. This imagery is powerful and directive, calling us to be beacons of hope and truth in a world often shrouded in deception and despair.

### Reflective Questions

1. Have you ever experienced a moment where you felt called to act in a crisis? What was that like?
2. Reflect on a time when a biblical prophecy or spiritual insight became suddenly clear or relevant to you. How did this change your perspective or actions?

3.  How can we, as modern believers, carry the **"burning lamps"** of faith and truth in today's world?
4.  In what ways can we prepare ourselves and others for the Lord's return, according to the lessons of history and scripture?
5.  What does it mean to you to be a **forerunner** in the context of your own spiritual journey and community?

## ACTIONABLE STEPS

- **Cultivate Readiness**: Immerse yourself in scripture and prayer, seeking to understand God's timing and purposes not just for the world, but for your life specifically.
- **Equip with Knowledge**: Stay informed about current events and historical parallels to discern the times, using wisdom to navigate complex situations with a biblical perspective.
- **Engage in Ministry**: Take active steps to share your faith and the urgency of the times with others, encouraging preparedness and spiritual vigilance in your community.

## JOURNALING **Prompt**

Reflect on the symbol of the burning lamp in your personal spiritual journey. What does it represent for you? How can you keep this lamp burning brightly in your life, ensuring you are ready and alert for whatever comes your way?

## CHAPTER 3

# INAUGURATION

**Be strong and courageous; do not be afraid nor dismayed, for the Lord your God is with you wherever you go. (Joshua 1:9 NKJV)**

In "Inauguration," we explore the critical intersection of "end times" and "real time," a juncture where prophetic events foretold in Scripture are unfolding before our eyes. The rebirth of Israel in 1948 serves as a profound marker, yet it is just one of many signs confirming that we are living in what the Bible describes as the "time of the end" (Daniel 12:4 NKJV). As events like Israel's wars and geopolitical shifts accelerate, they not only fulfill biblical prophecy but also underscore the urgency of our role in advancing God's Kingdom amidst these birth pangs.

This era is one of **unprecedented crossroads** in history, challenging every believer to discern the signs of the times accurately. The escalation of global crises—from cyber warfare affecting infrastructures like Key Bridge to societal upheavals due to compromised borders and the rise of global deception—

highlights the critical need for spiritual watchfulness. We find ourselves amid hypersonic threats, deep fakes, and the looming specter of technologies that could fulfill the prophecy of the mark of the beast, underscoring the reality of living in a time where **prophetic fulfillment** intertwines with everyday news.

As spiritual watchmen, Jolene and I, along with our counterparts in the intelligence community, face Armageddon-like scenarios with increasing frequency. These scenarios, which range from fabricated pandemics to orchestrated political chaos, point to a world teetering on the brink of prophetic culmination. This reality demands a **strategic prayer** and **prophetic ministry** that not only understands but actively engages in countering the antichrist agenda manifesting globally.

In response to these challenges, this book aims not just to inform but to equip. It is designed as a manual for living effectively in these end times, helping readers to align with God's timing, understand His prophetic calendar, and engage in transformative action. The **role of the believer** at this critical juncture is to be both watchful and proactive, ensuring that our responses are grounded in biblical prophecy and led by the Holy Spirit.

### REFLECTIVE QUESTIONS

1. How do current global events align with biblical prophecies you are aware of?
2. What role does strategic prayer play in your life as you navigate these end times?
3. How can we as believers ensure that our engagement in societal issues is both prophetic and effective?
4. In what ways has your understanding of the end times changed or deepened in recent years?

5. How do the challenges we face today compare to historical biblical challenges, such as those faced by Israel?

## Actionable Steps

- **Cultivate Awareness**: Regularly study prophetic Scriptures and current events to discern the times and prepare your heart and mind for action.
- **Equip with Prayer**: Develop a disciplined prayer routine that targets strategic areas revealed through prophecy and current global challenges.
- **Engage in Community**: Build relationships within a community of like-minded believers to strengthen your spiritual resilience and collective impact.

## Journaling Prompt

Reflect on the current global and local events. How do they make you feel about living in the end times? Journal about how you see God moving in these events and what actions He might be calling you to take as part of His strategic plan for this era.

# CHAPTER 4

# THE ARMAGEDDON CLOCK

**In times of uncertainty and upheaval, remember that God's timing is perfect and He has a plan for redemption. "But the end of all things is at hand; therefore be serious and watchful in your prayers." 1 Peter 4:7, NKJV**

In reflecting upon the **Significance of the Doomsday Clock**, we recognize the urgency with which our world teeters on the brink of profound change. The Doomsday Clock, as mentioned by Dr. Rachel Bronson, serves as a grim reminder of our global predicament, pushing us to consider the prophetic implications of our times. It's in these pivotal moments, while standing at Tel Megiddo, that the gravity of our situation becomes palpable. This ancient site, also known as Armageddon, is not just a tourist destination but a **Prophetic Setting at Tel Megiddo**, a crucial watchman's perch that has seen countless historical battles and is prophesied to see the ultimate confrontation in human history. The Bible vividly describes this location as the stage for the final battle in the book of Revelation, intertwining our spiritual heritage with the very real landscape before us.

During a visit to this profound site, the presence of God was palpable, contrasting sharply with the historical and future battles it signifies. It was here that Jolene received a profound **Vision of the Grandfather Clock** overlaying the Jezreel Valley. This vision, marking ten minutes to midnight, underscored the critical urgency of God's prophetic timeline, a divine alert to the imminent approach of pivotal events in the spiritual realm.

This vision became all the more significant when, months later, a conflict erupted, as if to echo the ticking of the prophetic clock. The **Recent Conflict and Its Implications** served as a somber reminder of the volatile world we inhabit. When Iran-proxy Hamas launched an attack, it was not just a regional conflict but a catalyst for a surge in global antisemitism, under-scoring the interconnectedness of modern geopolitical events and biblical prophecy.

Amidst these turbulent times, we are reminded of the impor-tance of aligning with God's calendar. The **Biblical Feasts as Time-keepers** are not mere religious observances but are imbued with deep prophetic significance, serving as markers and reminders of God's faithful interventions throughout history. Observing these feasts allows us to sync our lives with the rhythm of divine timing, drawing us closer to the heart of God and His plans for humanity.

The **Cyclical Nature of Hebraic Time** profoundly impacts our understanding of prophecy and our place within it. Time, from a Hebraic perspective, is not linear but cyclical, with events and themes recurring in a divine pattern that invites us to learn from the past to navigate the present and future. This cyclical pattern is vividly portrayed in the scriptures and is reflected in the recurring challenges and triumphs of God's people.

As we observe the unfolding of these prophetic signs, we

must also be wary of the **Antichrist Timing**. This malevolent force seeks to distort and manipulate God's timing to thwart the divine plan. Throughout society, we see the imposition of perverse timings that seek to desecrate what is holy and to hasten destruction and chaos.

Our understanding of God's communication through natural signs is further deepened as we consider the **Celestial Signs as Divine Messages**. The scriptures are rich with references to celestial events as signals from God, guiding and warning His people. These signs, from solar eclipses to blood moons, are not coincidental but are part of a divine language that speaks across the ages.

This call to spiritual vigilance is both personal and corporate. The narrative brings this home through a personal health scare and a national crisis, tying these events to a **Personal and Corporate Call to Action**. These challenges are not merely individual trials but are part of a broader divine call to repentance and alignment with God's covenantal purposes.

Ultimately, the chapter culminates in a powerful affirmation of **Restoration Through Covenant**. Just as God's covenant with His people has withstood the tests of time, so too does our opportunity for restoration through a renewed commitment to His ways. This restoration is not just a return to old paths but a profound transformation that aligns us with the divine rhythm of life and mission.

**REFLECTIVE QUESTIONS**

1. How does the symbolism of the Doomsday Clock affect your understanding of the urgency of current global events?

2. Reflect on the significance of Tel Megiddo (Armageddon) in biblical prophecy. Why do you think this specific location is emphasized in scripture?

3. In what ways does the vision of the grandfather clock challenge your perception of God's timing in your life?

4. Consider the impacts of global events like the conflict described. How do they reflect or distort biblical prophecies according to the chapter?

5. How can observing biblical feasts enhance your spiritual understanding and alignment with God's timing?

## ACTIONABLE STEPS

- **Cultivate Awareness**: Cultivate a deeper understanding of biblical prophecies and their relevance to current events. This can be done through study groups, sermons, and personal bible study.

- **Equip with Knowledge**: Equip yourself with knowledge about the significance of biblical feasts and celestial events. Learn how these can be used as tools for understanding divine messages and timings.

- **Engage in Reflection**: Engage in regular reflection and prayer about your role in God's prophetic timeline. Consider how you can align more closely with God's purposes through your daily choices and long-term commitments.

### Journaling **Prompt**

Reflect on the recent global events and their possible prophetic significance. How do these events challenge or reinforce your faith? Journal about ways you can actively seek to understand and align with God's timing in the midst of these events.

# CHAPTER 5
# SPIRIT OF ELIJAH

**Be strong and of good courage; do not be afraid, nor be dismayed, for the Lord your God is with you wherever you go. —Joshua 1:9 NKJV**

As we stood atop the summit of Armageddon, overlooking the Jezreel Valley, it became clear that the **Prophetic Vision and Action** required of us was set against a backdrop of immense biblical history and urgency. The vision of the giant clock was not just a symbol but a divine appointment for us to act, marking the midnight hour where significant shifts occur. This moment underscored the crucial timing of our mission—God's call was immediate and pressing.

Our journey to Israel was driven by a divine directive to **Consecrate for Service**, much like Gideon before us. God's instructions on the flight from Washington DC were clear: to consecrate ourselves afresh in preparation for the significant task at the Jordan River. This spiritual preparation was vital, mirroring Gideon's own rejection of idolatry, as we too were called to purify ourselves before engaging in the task of picking up the mantle of Elijah.

Our goal in traveling to Israel was inspired by a profound vision to **Pursue the Double Portion Mantle** of Elijah. The narrative of Elijah passing his mantle to Elisha by the Jordan River is a powerful testament to the transfer of spiritual authority. In 2014, during our annual Turnaround gathering, a flash vision revealed Jolene and me by the muddy banks of the Jordan, picking up Jewish prayer shawls that represented this double portion. This mantle was not just for us but was a significant empowerment intended for the broader body of Christ, symbolizing a pivotal moment for spiritual legacy and authority.

This mantle represents a **Covenant-Centric Turnaround Anointing** that is pivotal for awakening and advancing God's Kingdom. The spirit and power of Elijah, meant to repair hearts, families, churches, and even national economies, underpins every facet of Kingdom advancement. Such an anointing turns hearts towards God and each other, fulfilling the profound covenant promises depicted in scriptures.

In pursuing this mantle, I was confronted with the need for **Personal Humility in Prophetic Ministry**. Initially dismissing the importance of the vision due to spiritual pride, I was reminded through Jolene's wisdom that such pursuits are not for personal aggrandizement but are about the greater work in the body of Christ. This was a humbling realization, redirecting the focus from self to the communal and transformative impact of the prophetic action.

Our plans had to align with God's timing, which became evident when the dates for our actions changed, teaching us the lesson of **Divine Timing and Confirmation**. Initially planned for December 12, our prophetic action at the Jordan River was rescheduled to December 10—a change that was confirmed as divinely ordained through a prophecy by Chuck Pierce. This adjustment was a clear demonstration that God's plans are not bound by our expectations or schedules but require our flexibility and obedience.

The **Symbolic Actions at Significant Locations** such as the Jordan River and Gideon Springs were not just geographical choices but were deeply rooted in biblical significance. These locations enriched our mission, connecting us with the historical and spiritual narratives of those who had come before us, and anchoring our actions in a legacy of faith.

During this mission, we were astounded to meet others who were also called to similar prophetic actions. This communal experience underscored the **Impact of Prophetic Actions on Global Ministry**, as friends and fellow ministers joined us. This gathering was not just a personal or isolated event but a part of a global shift in the prophetic movement, marking a collective step forward in the spiritual realm.

Through Jolene's profound spiritual experiences during this journey, we were made acutely aware of the **Warnings of Upcoming Challenges**. She saw visions of severe challenges and shakings that both Israel and America were about to face. This revelation was daunting, reminding us of the weight of our prayers and the serious preparation needed to face these trials.

Lastly, the narrative of Elijah's bold confrontation with King Ahab gave us a vivid illustration of the **Role of Prophetic Authority in Governance**. Elijah's authority to declare drought over Israel as a judgment against Ahab's idolatry was a divine mandate that no earthly power could contest. This historical moment serves as a powerful reminder of the spiritual authority that God bestows upon His prophets, which transcends human governance and is directly accountable to God alone.

Through these experiences and revelations, the Spirit of Elijah teaches us about the power of divine callings and the responsibilities that come with them. As we engage with these truths, let us move forward with a heart attuned to God's timing, a spirit prepared for His work, and a humility that seeks to serve His purposes above all.

### REFLECTIVE QUESTIONS

1. What does the concept of the "double portion" of Elijah's mantle mean to you, and how can it apply to your spiritual life or ministry?
2. How can you personally engage in spiritual consecration to prepare for God's assignments, similar to how Jon and Jolene prepared before their prophetic action?
3. In what ways can you recognize and combat spiritual pride in your life, especially when engaged in ministry or spiritual activities?
4. How does the idea of divine timing change your perspective on waiting and acting on God's instructions? Can you recall a time when waiting on God proved to be beneficial in your own life?
5. What significance do you find in the locations chosen for prophetic actions in this chapter, and how do they enhance the narrative of God's ongoing work in the world today?

### ACTIONABLE STEPS

- **Cultivate a Heart of Consecration**: Regularly set aside times for fasting and prayer to cleanse and prepare your heart for receiving and carrying out God's plans.

- **Equip Yourself with Knowledge of God's Word**: Deepen your understanding of biblical stories and principles related to prophetic ministry, such as those of Elijah, Elisha, and Gideon, to better recognize and respond to God's voice.
- **Engage in Reflective Prayer**: Reflect on the areas in your life where you need a turnaround. Pray specifically for the restoration of relationships and alignment with God's will, just as the spirit of Elijah aims to restore and turn hearts.

JOURNALING **Prompt**

Reflect on a time when you felt called to a specific action or ministry. How did you discern it was God's voice? What steps did you take to obey, and what were the outcomes? Write about how this experience has shaped your understanding of God's guidance and timing in your life.

~

# CHAPTER 6
# SOUNDING FORTH THE TRUMPET

**Let us not become weary in doing good, for at the proper time we will reap a harvest if we do not give up. - Galatians 6:9 (NKJV)**

**"Watch and pray, lest you enter into temptation. The spirit indeed is willing, but the flesh is weak." - Matthew 26:41 (NKJV)**

In the poignant echoes of history, where the past reverberates with urgent lessons for today, I invite you to grasp the deep **resonance of the past in present calls**. As we stood in the solemnity of Yad Vashem, the sound of the shofar —a ram's horn traditionally used in Jewish religious ceremonies —rang out. This was no ordinary call; it was imbued with the profound symbolism of the "Lion of Judah," urging us to remember and act against the echoes of tyranny. This moment underscores not only a historical reflection but also a vigorous call to vigilance. It connects the tragic atrocities of the Holocaust with our ongoing struggle against antisemitism and authoritarian tendencies that sadly, still surface in our time.

The **symbolism of the shofar** in this context extends beyond its biblical roots, becoming a clarion call to action. It is a powerful reminder of our duty to remember and respond to injustice. As the shofar sounded that day, it seemed to cut through the ages, linking us with generations past and calling us to stand guard over the values we hold dear. It is more than a ritual; it is a summons to awaken our collective conscience and stand vigilant against the resurgence of hatred and division.

Our journey through Israel was marked by profound **link between historical events and prophetic insights**. From the streets of Ein Kerem to the somber halls of Yad Vashem, every site visited and every scripture reflected upon reinforced the continuity of divine messaging. As we retraced the steps of prophets and witnessed the landscapes of biblical tales, we were reminded that the words of the prophets are not confined to the dusty pages of history. They are alive, resonating through the ages, and eerily relevant to our current geopolitical and spiritual climate.

In understanding the **importance of commemoration and remembrance**, our visit to Yad Vashem was pivotal. This hallowed place does more than chronicle the horrors of the past; it challenges us to apply its lessons today. As we walked through exhibits of personal artifacts—torah scrolls, violins, and children's storybooks—it was a poignant reminder that these were not just items; they were fragments of lives interrupted. Commemorating these lives compels us to defend the truth and ensures that the seeds of such atrocities find no fertile ground in our times.

The narratives shared and the places visited wove together a tapestry of **prophetic warnings and modern realities**. Dreams and visions recounted by members of our group were not dismissed as mere figments of imagination but were considered as divine alerts. These prophetic insights, particularly concerning the resurgence of movements akin to past atrocities, highlighted the necessity for spiritual and practical readiness. It's unsettling how the threads of history and prophecy intertwine, revealing patterns that recur with alarming regularity.

One of the most stirring accounts was the story of an American POW during WWII, which profoundly illustrated the **power of unity in facing adversity**. In a defiant act of solidarity, he proclaimed, "We are all Jews here!" when confronted by Nazi soldiers demanding the segregation of Jewish prisoners. This moment of courage is a stark reminder of the strength that lies in unity. It is a call for us to embody the same spirit of solidarity when faced with modern-day injustices, recognizing that our collective action can thwart the plans of oppressors.

Reflecting on the land of Israel, its beauty, and its burdens, one cannot overlook its **spiritual significance**. This land is not just a place of historical and cultural interest; it is prophetic ground zero. The biblical prophecies that speak of Israel's central role in the end times come to life as we walk its paths. This awareness should shape our perception of global events and our responses to them, as we see the unfolding of scriptural truths in current headlines.

Our observations of the political landscape highlighted a critical modern concern—the **impact of political divisions on national security**. Israel's internal conflicts serve as a stark example of how domestic strife can erode a nation's external strength. These divisions not only weaken a nation but also embolden its adversaries. As we witnessed the spirited debates and protests, it became clear that unity is not just idealistic but essential for survival.

Throughout our journey, the call to be prophetic voices in our times was ever-present. We are urged to **call for a prophetic**

**response to current challenges**, recognizing the times and knowing what to do, much like the sons of Issachar in biblical times. This prophetic engagement involves discerning the signs of the times and responding with wisdom and courage. It's not enough to be passive observers; we are called to be active participants in God's unfolding plan.

Lastly, the personal stories shared, the dreams recounted, and the collective experiences we encountered all culminated in an **encouragement of personal spiritual vigilance**. Each of us is called to be vigilant in prayer, tuned to God's directions, and prepared to act on the insights we receive. This vigilance is not borne out of fear but out of a commitment to be God's instruments of peace and justice in a world that desperately needs both.

In this chapter, we traverse a landscape that is both historical and prophetic, personal and communal, urging each of us to heed the call of the shofar—not just as a sound echoing through the corridors of Yad Vashem but as a perpetual call to action in our lives today.

### REFLECTIVE QUESTIONS

1. How can the historical use of the shofar as a call to action inspire modern responses to injustice and evil?
2. In what ways does remembering past atrocities like the Holocaust impact your perspective on current global issues?
3. How do you perceive the role of prophecy in today's world, especially in relation to geopolitical events and spiritual warnings?
4. What lessons can be drawn from the unity and courage shown by figures like Master Sgt. Roddie

Edmonds during WWII in today's context of rising antisemitism and division?

5. How do you engage with the concept of Israel's prophetic significance, and how does this shape your views on international relations and spiritual responsibilities?



- **Cultivate Awareness and Remembrance**: Engage in learning about historical events like the Holocaust and their implications today to foster a culture of remembrance and resistance against tyranny.
- **Equip Yourself with Prophetic Insight**: Regularly seek to understand and discern the times through prayer, study of the Scriptures, and attention to prophetic voices, preparing yourself spiritually for the challenges of the times.
- **Engage in Advocacy and Support**: Actively participate in movements or organizations that combat antisemitism and support the rights and safety of marginalized communities, reflecting your commitment to justice and unity.

JOURNALING **Prompt**

Reflect on a time when you felt called to stand up against an injustice. What were the challenges, and how did you respond? How can this experience inform your future actions in similar circumstances?

# CHAPTER 7
# COME UP HIGHER—EXITING THE X

**Let us not become weary in doing good, for at the proper time we will reap a harvest if we do not give up. - Galatians 6:9 (NKJV)**

**"Watch and pray, lest you enter into temptation. The spirit indeed is willing, but the flesh is weak." - Matthew 26:41 (NKJV)**

In this chapter, we explore pivotal moments that beckon us to a higher calling amid global and personal crises. From the Armageddon clock striking midnight for Israel and America to the prophetic urgency ignited by the Spirit of Elijah, our journey has reached a critical juncture. The **global release of the spirit and power of Elijah** was confirmed astonishingly by the hand of God, aligning biblical prophecy with our modern struggles against dark forces intent on silencing the divine call.

The gift of a cherished shofar at Yad Vashem became a **symbol of divine alarm,** not just over imminent wars but also against a rising wave of global antisemitism. This alarming resurgence, especially on liberal college campuses across the US, defies understanding and challenges us to respond with informed, spirited resistance. The X Eclipse over the 2024 election year sharpened the focus on these dark forces attempting to X-out our nation, echoing Cindy Jacobs' longstanding prophetic warning.

As we witness **horrific sins by trusted leaders** within the body of Christ, the feeling of disenfranchisement grows among believers, challenging our faith and resolve. This chapter underscores the importance of wrestling through these events with the Lord, strengthening us to **navigate future challenges** with fortified faith and unwavering commitment.

**Hebrew cyclical time** theory suggests that events we experience now will recur with greater intensity, a concept that prepares us to face accelerated end-times scenarios with a proactive, spiritually enlightened stance. Through this understanding, we see the unfolding of prophetic times in Israel, America, and the world, urging us to remain vigilant and prepared.

The stark reminder of **God's unchanging love** amidst these trials reorients us to our foundational belief: Jesus remains our real-time Redeemer and soon-coming King. This acknowledgment serves as a bedrock as we face the shifting sands of societal and spiritual upheaval.

An urgent call to action resonates through the shofar's blast, a real-time trumpet speaking Revelation's words: "Come up here, and I will show you what must take place…" This summons to **ascend spiritually and morally** invites us to view our challenges from a higher vantage point, where spiritual insights can transform our earthly responses.

The **moral and spiritual ascension** necessary for these end times requires us to adopt a heavenly perspective, positioning ourselves with Christ in the spiritual realms while maintaining the moral high ground in our earthly engagements. This dual positioning is crucial for overcoming the dark forces arrayed against us.

**John's ascension** serves as a model for our own spiritual journey. Just as John ascended to receive Revelation's visions, we too are called to elevate our spiritual understanding and readiness, ensuring we are prepared for what lies ahead.

Our proximity to alarms, both literal and spiritual, underscores the immediacy of God's warnings. From alarms sounding across cities to the personal, pressing alerts in our lives, these signs are God's way of emphasizing the urgency of our times, compelling us to **heed His call to come up higher**.

**REFLECTIVE QUESTIONS**

1. How can the global release of the spirit and power of Elijah inspire you to engage more deeply with your spiritual calling?

2. In what ways does the symbolism of the shofar as a divine alarm affect your perspective on global events and your personal spiritual vigilance?

3. Reflect on a time when you felt a profound shift in your understanding of God's timing. How did this insight change your approach to spiritual and daily challenges?

4. Considering the cyclical nature of Hebrew time, how do you prepare for the challenges that may recur with greater intensity?

5. What does it mean to you to "come up higher" in both spiritual and moral terms? How can this perspective shift influence your actions and decisions?

. . .

**ACTIONABLE STEPS**

- **Cultivate a Prophetic Perspective**: Regularly engage with scripture and prophetic teachings to understand the signs of the times and how they relate to current global and personal events.
- **Equip Yourself for Spiritual Warfare**: Enhance your spiritual practices—such as prayer, fasting, and scriptural study—to strengthen your spiritual resilience against the forces of darkness.
- **Engage in Community and Accountability**: Foster relationships with fellow believers who can support, encourage, and hold you accountable in your spiritual journey, especially in times of crisis or confusion.

**JOURNALING Prompt**

Reflect on how the current global crises and personal challenges have impacted your spiritual life. What changes have you felt compelled to make? How has your understanding of God's call for you to "come up higher" evolved during these times?

43

## CHAPTER 8

# TESHUVAH

**Return to the stronghold, you prisoners of hope. Even today I declare that I will restore double to you. — Zechariah 9:12 NKJV**

In this chapter, I invite you to explore the profound concept of **Teshuvah**, a Hebrew term meaning repentance or return. This call to repentance is not merely a theological abstract but a direct divine invitation for us to ascend spiritually by aligning more closely with God's will. The Lord's call for the IHOPKC movement and the broader Christian community to return to covenant faithfulness underpins the urgent need for purity in our lives, especially as we prepare for the end times.

The dream I share in this narrative is not just a personal revelation but a symbolic depiction for the church at large. In this dream, Cathy, whose name signifies **Purity and Repentance**, lights a candle on a sparsely filled stage and weeps as she utters the word "Teshuvah." This poignant scene serves as a powerful reminder that purity and a contrite heart are essential for true spiritual renewal and revival within our communities.

The seasonal timing of this call to repentance is significant as it aligns with the Jewish High Holy Days, specifically **Rosh Hashanah and Yom Kippur**. These days are not merely cultural observances but carry deep spiritual significance, marking times when God examines our lives and writes His verdicts for the coming year. It is during these days that we are called to reflect deeply on our actions, seek forgiveness, and commit to personal and communal transformation.

The concept of **Global and Biblical Implications** of repentance is crucial as it extends beyond individual actions to encompass global spiritual dynamics. Our repentance is intricately linked to prophetic events and the ultimate return of Christ. This chapter underscores that the practice of teshuvah is not an isolated act but a critical element in the redemptive drama of human history, highlighting our role in God's cosmic narrative.

Addressing **Personal and Corporate Responsibility**, I reflect on the broader implications of our spiritual actions. The prophetic word given to the leadership of the IHOPKC and extended to the global church is a clarion call to assess our roles within God's kingdom critically. Each of us bears the weight of influencing not only our own spiritual journeys but also the collective spiritual health of our communities.

We delve into practical steps through **Seven Steps to Practicing Teshuvah**. These steps provide a framework for engaging with God and our community in a meaningful way. From self-examination to making amends, each step is designed to guide us through a process of genuine repentance and spiritual renewal.

Forgiveness is more than a religious concept; it is a gateway to spiritual freedom. In **Forgiveness as Freedom**, we explore how forgiving others liberates us from the chains of past offenses and aligns us with God's law of love. This act of letting go not only heals us but also restores our relationships and communities.

King David's life offers timeless lessons on covenant faithfulness and the power of repentance. His experiences teach us that **David's Example of Covenant and Repentance** is pivotal in understanding how our actions resonate within the broader context of God's mercy and judgment. David's story is a testament to the fact that God's compassion is available to those who earnestly seek forgiveness and strive to restore their covenant relationship with Him.

As we approach the **End Times and Final Redemption**, it becomes clear that the principles of teshuvah will play a significant role in the unfolding of prophetic events. This realization should not incite fear but rather inspire a committed effort toward spiritual preparedness and integrity, knowing that our actions contribute to the redemption narrative foretold in Scripture.

In writing this chapter, my aim has been to draw each of us into a deeper understanding of our need for repentance and the urgency of responding to God's call. As we engage with these principles, let us be mindful of the transformative power of **Teshuvah** and embrace it not only as a duty but as a privilege to come up higher and closer to the heart of God.


**REFLECTIVE QUESTIONS**

1. Reflect on a time when you felt called to repentance. How did acknowledging your shortcomings before God change your relationship with Him and others?
2. Considering the concept of 'teshuvah,' how can you actively return to a path of righteousness in areas where you've strayed?

3. How does the example of King David inspire you to handle personal failures and seek restoration?
4. What steps can you take to foster a spirit of forgiveness in your community, mirroring the forgiveness that God offers us?
5. How can understanding the Jewish High Holy Days enrich your Christian faith and understanding of God's calendar and timing?

**ACTIONABLE STEPS**

- **Cultivate a Heart of Repentance**: Begin each day with a prayer of repentance, asking God to reveal areas of your life that need alignment with His will. This daily practice cultivates a heart sensitive to the Holy Spirit's guidance.
- **Equip Yourself with Forgiveness**: Study biblical teachings on forgiveness and actively practice forgiving those who have wronged you, recognizing this as a vital step in your spiritual armor against bitterness and resentment.
- **Engage in Community Restoration**: Initiate or participate in a community outreach program that focuses on reconciliation and healing, using your testimony and lessons learned from the principles of teshuvah to inspire others.

**JOURNALING Prompt**

Reflect on the areas in your life where you need to enact teshuvah. Consider the steps towards repentance you've taken and those you still need to take. How can you align these actions with the scriptural call to return to God's covenant? Write down your thoughts and any scriptures that come to mind during this reflection.

CHAPTER 9

# RESCUING YOUR LAMPSTAND

**"Don't let my love grow cold. I'm calling out, light the fire again! Don't let my vision die. I'm calling out, light the fire again!" — "Light the Fire Again" lyrics, Brian Doerksen**

**"The Year 2025 is the Year of the Lampstand—the rescued lampstand, says the Lord!"**

On a crisp autumn morning at a cabin overlooking the Allegheny River, these words awakened me with a profound revelation. The spirit of revival is stirring, and the Lord is calling us to rescue the lampstands of our hearts —those places within us that have dimmed under life's pressures and challenges. This chapter unfolds the mystery of the biblical lampstand and invites us to rekindle our first love with Christ.

The **lampstand** in Scripture symbolizes our spirit's bright burning light, representing our passion and love for Jesus. Just as a lampstand holds a flame, our hearts hold the flame of our love

51

and devotion to God. This year, God is reigniting diminished flames and setting our spirits ablaze anew.

When I mention the **spirit of Elijah**, I am referring to a movement of boldness and restoration sweeping across the land, reminiscent of Elijah's powerful ministry that called Israel back to God. This movement is about turning hearts back to God and restoring broken relationships—between individuals and the divine, and within communities.

The rescue of our lampstand is akin to reigniting a fire that has nearly gone out. Many of us feel our spiritual vigor waning after enduring personal trials or navigating the complexities of life. Yet, Jesus is moving powerfully to restore this fire, ensuring that our love and devotion do not grow cold even in the challenging midnight hours of our lives.

**Rescuing the Fire of First Love** is essential because it reconnects us with our foundational reasons for faith—the love and awe of Jesus that initially drew us to Him. Just as Revelation warns, leaving our first love can lead to our lampstands being removed, symbolizing a loss of God's presence and power in our lives.

In the journey of faith, we often encounter seasons that test our fervor and commitment. The pressures of life, misunderstandings about God's character, or disillusionments within church communities can dim our spiritual light. Yet, this chapter guides us through **ten proven steps to recover your fire**, ensuring that our hearts remain aflame with love for God and His purposes.

Our love for God is deeply personal and transformative, yet it is also constantly under assault by forces that seek to diminish its brightness. The admonition from Revelation about **losing our first love** highlights the critical need to actively maintain our passion for God through intentional practices that keep our spiritual fervor alive.

**Breaking Up with Jesus** discusses a symbolic low point in our relationship with God, where disillusionment or fatigue might lead us to question our closeness with Him. This narrative isn't just about temporary spiritual lapses; it's about understanding that Jesus' commitment to us remains steadfast, even when our focus wavers.

The steps to **Rescuing Your Lampstand** involve practical, heartfelt actions that bring us back to our first encounters with God's love. These actions rekindle our spiritual fervor and realign our lives with God's purposes. They ensure that our lampstands, our central spiritual essence, are firmly rooted in the love and power of Jesus.

### REFLECTIVE QUESTIONS

1. Reflect on your initial encounters with God's love. How has your passion for prayer, worship, and the Word shifted over time?
2. What does the imagery of a lampstand evoke in your spiritual life? How can you see this concept influencing your daily walk with God?
3. In what ways have you felt your spiritual fervor diminish? What circumstances or challenges have contributed to this feeling?
4. How do you resonate with the idea of 'rescuing your lampstand'? What steps can you take to ensure your spiritual fire is continually rekindled?
5. Reflect on the role of repentance in maintaining your lampstand. How does turning back to God renew your spiritual vitality?

**ACTIONABLE STEPS**

- **Cultivate Daily Engagement with Scripture**: Commit to reading and meditating on the Bible every day. Let the Word of God be the oil that keeps your lamp burning brightly.
- **Equip Yourself with Prayer**: Set dedicated times for prayer. Use this time not just for requests, but for cultivating a deeper relationship with Jesus, allowing Him to fill you with His love and peace.
- **Engage in Community Worship**: Regularly participate in community worship settings. These gatherings can significantly boost your spiritual vitality and help maintain the flame of your lampstand.

**JOURNALING Prompt**

Reflect on the current state of your spiritual lampstand. What actions can you take to ensure it remains bright and burning? Write about the times when you felt closest to God and what activities or behaviors characterized those periods. How can you reintegrate these practices into your current spiritual routine?

~

# CHAPTER 10

# COME UP HIGHER— BEFORE HIS FACE

God's call to "come up higher" is an invitation into a deeper, more profound relationship with Him. As you ascend spiritually, you are positioned to receive greater revelations and empowered to act effectively on His behalf in this world.

**"But you are come unto mount Sion, and unto the city of the living God, the heavenly Jerusalem, and to an innumerable company of angels," (Hebrews 12:22 NKJV).**

In this transformative journey of faith, we are invited by God to ascend spiritually and embrace a **Elevated Perspective through Repentance**. When we humble ourselves and turn from our ways, God promises to lift us up and reveal aspects of His glory previously hidden from our eyes. This process is not merely about feeling remorseful but about undergoing a change that shifts our spiritual outlook, aligning us more closely with God's divine perspective.

As we delve deeper into our relationship with the Lord, we hear the call, as John did in the book of Revelation, to **Come Up**

**Higher**. This isn't just a physical elevation but a spiritual one, where we are summoned to a realm that offers a clearer, more profound revelation of God's plans and purposes. In these higher realms of spiritual engagement, hidden truths of the divine become unveiled, and we gain a richer understanding of who God is and what He intends for our lives and the world around us.

One profound aspect of our spiritual journey involves being sent on a mission, not just anywhere, but specifically **Before His Face**. This signifies a position of favor and closeness, preparing us for impactful ministry. By being sent before His face, we are first drawn into an intimate encounter with Christ, which then propels us into our God-given missions with a heart fully aligned with His purposes.

In these divine encounters, we grasp the **Essence of the Forerunner Calling**. The call to be a forerunner is about more than just pioneering; it's about being propelled by an intimate relationship with Jesus. This primary calling of encountering Jesus equips us to carry out our secondary calling—impacting cities and nations with the gospel. It ensures that our actions and ministry flow from a heart that is in tune with God's heartbeat.

Our engagement with God's divine authority becomes evident as we witness the **Authority in Real Time**. Elijah's boldness in confronting Ahab wasn't from his own strength but was a direct result of his standing "before the Lord." This authority is not just historical; it's available to us today as we stand before God, receiving real-time mandates that empower us to speak and act with divine authority.

God continually invites us into His presence, urging us to engage with Him in His **Throne Room**. This isn't a mere ceremonial visit; it's an ongoing interaction where we gain insights and directives for earthly governance. These throne room encounters are meant to influence earthly realities, allowing us to enforce heavenly decisions on earth, thereby manifesting God's kingdom here and now.

A key to manifesting God's kingdom on earth is recognizing that it is accomplished **By My Spirit**. This phrase, echoed from Zechariah, emphasizes that our efforts in God's kingdom are not to be by human might or power but through the Spirit's enablement. This divine empowerment equips us to fulfill our calling and ensures that our endeavors are aligned with God's will and executed in His strength.

Our participation in divine governance is further deepened as we find ourselves **Engaging with the Spiritual Council**. Like Jeremiah and Elijah, we are called to stand in God's council, receiving strategic divine communications. This engagement is not just for our personal guidance but is crucial for making impactful decisions that align with God's will for communities and nations.

The **Covenantal Authority** that we hold as believers is foundational to our role in God's kingdom. This authority is based on our covenant relationship with Christ, establishing us in specific areas of influence. As we understand and exercise this covenantal authority, we align closer with God's governmental structure, bringing His rule and reign into the environments He has assigned to us.

Lastly, the journey culminates as we **Secure Our Spiritual Seat**. This concept involves more than just understanding our authority; it requires us to actively take up our position in Christ. This means overcoming personal trials and aligning closely with God's statutes, which mirrors the journey of biblical figures who received authority after proving their faithfulness to God's commands.

In summary, our ascent in the spiritual realms is not just about personal growth but about embracing the fullness of what

God has called us to be and do. By ascending higher, engaging before His face, and exercising the authority granted to us, we are equipped to impact the world effectively, ushering in the realities of God's kingdom on earth as it is in heaven.

## REFLECTIVE QUESTIONS

1. What does "coming up higher" mean in your personal spiritual journey, and how can you actively respond to this divine invitation?
2. How does understanding the role of being sent 'before His face' change your perception of ministry or daily living as a Christian?
3. In what ways can you cultivate a closer relationship with the Holy Spirit to ensure your efforts in ministry or daily decisions are Spirit-led?
4. How can standing in the council of the Lord alter your approach to spiritual responsibilities or leadership within your community?
5. What are some practical steps you can take to secure your spiritual seat of authority and increase your effectiveness as a Kingdom influencer?

## ACTIONABLE STEPS

- **Cultivate a Repentant Heart**
- Regularly engage in personal reflection and repentance to maintain a pure heart and a clear spiritual perspective. This prepares you to ascend spiritually and receive fresh revelations from God.

- **Equip Yourself with Knowledge of God's Word**
- Deepen your understanding of biblical teachings on authority, the role of the Holy Spirit, and God's kingdom principles. This knowledge will empower you to stand confidently in your assigned role within God's plans.
- **Engage in Consistent Prayer and Worship**
- Commit to a disciplined prayer life and regular worship, which are essential for accessing God's throne room. This will help you to receive timely guidance and the spiritual strength needed to execute your divine mandate.

JOURNALING **Prompt**

Reflect on a recent time when you felt a spiritual "summons" to come up higher in your walk with God. What were the circumstances, and how did you respond? What changes did you notice in your spiritual life as a result?

∾

# CHAPTER II

# THE MIDNIGHT RIDERS: FORERUNNER MINISTRY IN THE END TIMES

In the quiet of the night, just as Paul Revere once did, we are called to a watchful readiness, anticipating the directives of Heaven. Like those vigilant few by Gideon's side, may we too remain alert, with our eyes on the horizon, ready to act upon the revelations given to us from the Throne Room.

**"Watch therefore, for you know neither the day nor the hour in which the Son of Man is coming." (Matthew 25:13 NKJV)**

In a world teeming with distractions and the clamor of life, the narrative of **The Midnight Riders: Forerunner Ministry in the End Times** draws us into the quiet urgency of a midnight call. As modern-day forerunners, we're entrusted with the mantle of readiness, a continuous vigil in the spiritual night that precedes the dawn. This call to vigilance is not born of fear but of a profound responsibility to be the bearers of light in increasing darkness.

Living with a **Strategic Positioning** akin to that of a

watchman across from the Pentagon underscores the necessity of understanding the times and being prepared for action. Just as intelligence officers assess threats and strategize responses, so must we discern the spiritual landscapes and ready ourselves for divine assignments. Our positions, though often unseen, are critical to the kingdom's advancements.

Drawing from historical and biblical insights, we learn that **Real-Time Intelligence** like that of Paul Revere's legendary ride is crucial. In spiritual terms, this involves an acute awareness of God's movements and the shifts in spiritual realms. Real-time intelligence from the Holy Spirit enables us to act swiftly and effectively, countering threats and seizing divine opportunities.

**The Midnight Cry** serves as a prophetic symbol of our times, a call to awaken from complacency and to arm ourselves with spiritual diligence. It's a stirring reminder that, like the ten virgins in Matthew 25, our lamps should be filled and our hearts ready for the Bridegroom's return. This cry isn't just a warning; it's an invitation to participate actively in God's unfolding plan.

Central to our calling is **Navigating Midnight Crises**, which are increasingly evident in our world today. From global upheavals to personal trials, these crises require a foundation of faith and a network of supportive, prayerful connections. Understanding these times and knowing how to pray effectively through them are marks of a true forerunner.

**Spiritual Readiness** is not a passive state but a dynamic engagement. It involves equipping ourselves with the Word, deepening our prayer lives, and fostering community connections that strengthen our spiritual resolve. This readiness empowers us to respond not just with physical actions but with spiritual authority that can shift atmospheres and open heavenly realms.

**Engaging in Heavenly Councils** provides the strategic

directives we need. Like the biblical prophets, gaining access to God's council through relentless prayer and intimacy with the Holy Spirit allows us to bring down strategies and wisdom that are not of this world. This engagement is crucial for leading effectively and stewarding the mysteries of God.

**Divine Turnarounds** are often birthed in the darkest hours. Our commitment to stand in the gap, to declare and enforce Heaven's rulings on earth, can lead to significant breakthroughs and shifts in spiritual territories. These turnarounds are testimonies of God's power to redeem and transform even the most dire situations.

As we **Prepare the Way of the Lord**, our actions and prayers pave the path for spiritual awakenings and revivals. This preparation is both a personal purification and a communal rallying call to align with God's purposes, ensuring that when He moves, we are moving in sync with His heart and mandate.

Lastly, **The Bridal Paradigm** underpins our mission. We are preparing not just for a series of events but for a wedding—the ultimate union of Christ with His purified bride. This perspective shifts our focus from mere earthly survival to preparing ourselves and others for an eternal communion with our King.

These insights lead us to a deeper engagement, a more profound waiting, and an active participation in the unfolding divine narrative. Our readiness and response can indeed shift the course of history, aligning it with the purposes of Heaven.

**REFLECTIVE QUESTIONS**

1. How has the concept of being a 'midnight rider' or forerunner changed your understanding of your spiritual responsibilities?

2. What strategies have you implemented to enhance your spiritual readiness for the 'midnight crises'?
3. In what ways do you engage with the heavenly council, and how has it impacted your ministry or personal life?
4. Can you identify a recent divine turnaround in your life or community that resulted from prayerful vigilance?
5. How does the bridal paradigm shift your perspective on your daily walk and spiritual readiness?

### ACTIONABLE STEPS

- **Cultivate Spiritual Vigilance** Commit to daily devotions and prayer that focus on listening and responding to the Holy Spirit. This daily discipline prepares you to act swiftly and effectively when God calls.
- **Equip with the Word and Fellowship** Regularly study scripture and engage in community with like-minded believers to sharpen your spiritual discernment and strengthen your faith foundation.
- **Engage in Prophetic Intercession** Participate in or initiate prayer gatherings that focus on interceding for your community, nation, and the global church. These sessions are vital for fostering spiritual readiness and enacting divine strategies.

**JOURNALING Prompt**

Reflect on a time when you felt particularly called to 'watch and pray.' How did this experience change your perception of spiritual readiness? What did you learn about God's timing and your role as a forerunner in His kingdom?

# CHAPTER 12

# THE HARVEST WARS: OVERCOMING END-TIME IDOLATRY

Remember, the battle is not yours, but God's. Stand firm in faith and in the power of His might, knowing that "He who is in you is greater than he who is in the world."

**"Yet in all these things we are more than conquerors through Him who loved us." - Romans 8:37 NKJV**

In this pivotal chapter, we explore the **Great Return to God,** a prophetic shift where multitudes are turning away from the seductions of modern idolatries—akin to Jezebel's table—and returning to the pure worship and reverence of the Lord. This renaissance is not merely a revival of religious fervor but a profound realignment with the divine principles that govern our lives and our nations. It mirrors the biblical narrative where Elijah stood boldly against the corrupt powers of his day, challenging us to do the same in our times.

We find ourselves in a relentless battle against **Antichrist Ideologies.** From ancient Baal worship to today's secular idols, these forces are at work, undermining the spiritual and moral fibers of our societies. The name Jezebel historically symbolizes such decay, her story reflecting the pervasive spread of idolatry and moral corruption. Today, these battles are not confined to the pages of scripture but unfold in the halls of our governments, our schools, and in the marketplace of ideas, where truth is often sacrificed on the altars of convenience and political correctness.

The call to spiritual warfare, to engage in **Harvest Wars**, is urgent. Our struggle is not against flesh and blood but against rulers, authorities, and powers of this dark world. As in the days of Elijah, who declared a divine drought against an ungodly regime, we too are called to pronounce God's truth against modern-day Jezebels and Ahabs, who propagate falsehood and lead many astray. This engagement is crucial for the preservation of our spiritual heritage and the future of our nations.

Reflecting on **Elijah's Prophetic Model**, we see a blueprint for our spiritual engagement. Elijah's confrontation with Ahab was not just about proving God's power but about calling a nation back to righteousness. In the same way, our actions, prayers, and declarations have profound implications, not just for personal piety but for national and global transformation.

The influence of **Jezebel's Influence Today** is alarmingly relevant. Like the ancient queen who spread idolatry through Israel, today's cultural forces seek to dilute and destroy the Judeo-Christian values foundational to our societies. This spirit is manifest in the relentless push for policies and practices that stand in stark opposition to God's commands, promoting a culture of idolatry and immorality that rivals the days of Jezebel.

In this context, the importance of **Restoration of Godly Values** cannot be overstated. We stand at the threshold of a Third Great Awakening, a divine opportunity to restore the altars of truth and righteousness in our hearts and communities. This awakening is about more than revival; it is about reformation—

realigning our laws, our cultural norms, and our personal lives with the will of God as revealed in Scripture.

Understanding the **Economic and Ecological Impact of Spiritual Actions** offers us insight into how our spiritual obedience or disobedience can affect more than our personal lives. Just as Elijah's proclamation of drought led to economic hardship, our moral and spiritual decisions have tangible impacts on our economies and environments. When we align with God's ways, we invite His blessing, not only on our souls but on our lands and livelihoods.

The narrative of Naboth's vineyard serves as a poignant reminder of the **Prophetic Destiny and National Heritage** that God has entrusted to us. Naboth refused to give up his inheritance, representing a steadfast commitment to divine destiny that we too must emulate. Our national and spiritual inheritances are under assault by modern-day Ahabs and Jezebels, who seek to usurp God's plans for our lives and lands. We must stand firm as Naboth did, refusing to surrender our heritage for the fleeting pleasures of sin.

The theme of **Covenantal Relationships** runs deep, as we are reminded that our alliances should reflect our heavenly citizenship. Just as Ahab's alignment with Jezebel brought calamity upon Israel, our partnerships and agreements—both personal and national—should be scrutinized for their fidelity to God's covenant. Our alliances must not be with the powers of this world but with the Kingdom of God, which offers life and peace.

As we engage in this sacred struggle, the call to **Global Impact of Local Faithfulness** is clear. Each act of obedience, each moment of truth-telling, each stand against injustice has ripple effects that can alter the course of history. Our local faithfulness to God's commands can shift national policies and influence global directions, ushering in an era of righteousness and peace that the prophets foresaw.

. . .

## Reflective Questions

1. What modern-day idols can be compared to Jezebel's table in your community or nation? How are they diverting people from God?
2. Reflect on a time when you witnessed a "drought" in your spiritual life. What brought restoration?
3. How can the story of Elijah's confrontation with Ahab and Jezebel guide your prayers for your nation's leaders?
4. In what ways can you personally contribute to a "Great Return" to godly values in your community?
5. How does the concept of spiritual warfare influence your understanding of global and local news events?

## Actionable Steps

- **Cultivate an Elijah-like Boldness**: Cultivate a spirit of boldness in your prayer life, asking God for the courage to stand against modern-day idolatries and injustices, much like Elijah did against Ahab and Jezebel.
- **Equip with Knowledge of the Word**: Equip yourself with a deep understanding of the Scriptures concerning idolatry, covenant, and prophetic destiny to discern and combat the spiritual influences that oppose God's plans for your community.
- **Engage in Community Transformation**: Engage actively in community or church initiatives that aim

to address and rectify moral and spiritual declines. Be a voice that promotes biblical values and covenantal living in public forums and discussions.

75

### Journaling **Prompt**

Reflect on the current "Harvest Wars" within your own life or community. Where do you see the influence of modern-day "Jezebels"? How can you, like Elijah, be an instrument of God's justice and righteousness in these situations?

~

# CHAPTER 13

# END-TIMES TREACHERY AND TRICKERY

Stand firm in your faith and be courageous; do not be afraid or dismayed. For the Lord your God is with you wherever you go. He will not fail you or forsake you even in the midst of deception and betrayal.

**"Have I not commanded you? Be strong and of good courage; do not be afraid, nor be dismayed, for the Lord your God is with you wherever you go." - Joshua 1:9 NKJV**

In our journey through "End-Times Treachery and Trickery," we delve into the complex dynamics of deceit that challenge our spiritual and communal life. Our exploration is not just to inform but to arm you with wisdom and proactive strategies against the spiritual warfare waged through deception.

We begin by defining the **Definition and Impact of Treachery and Trickery**. Understanding these terms is essential as they form the foundation of many conflicts both in personal realms and wider community interactions. Treachery cuts deeply, involving betrayal from those we trust. It breaks the foundational trust that bonds relationships, leading to profound emotional and spiritual turmoil. Trickery, by its nature, involves cunning deceptions aimed at misleading individuals to believe falsehoods, thereby manipulating actions to the deceiver's advantage. Both are potent tools used by adversaries to destabilize the faithful and corrupt the unsuspecting.

Drawing from **Historical and Modern Parallels**, we see how these deceptions have not only shaped historical outcomes but continue to influence modern-day scenarios. From the treachery that led to major political upheavals to trickery in financial scams, understanding these patterns equips us with the foresight to recognize and counteract similar strategies in our times.

The scriptures provide rich insights, as **Biblical Examples** of deceit and its consequences are prolific. From the betrayal of Jesus by Judas to the deceit Jacob practiced on Esau, these stories are not mere narratives. They serve as profound lessons on the spiritual, emotional, and sometimes physical consequences of deceit, guiding us in forging paths of integrity.

In today's context, **Modern Manifestations** of treachery and trickery are rampant in digital misinformation, corporate espionage, and even within personal relationships. Recognizing these can help us navigate our interactions with a guarded yet open heart, balancing trust with wisdom.

Understanding treachery and trickery as tools in **Spiritual Warfare** emphasizes the need for spiritual armor. Paul's letters to the Ephesians highlight the necessity of wearing the full armor of God to stand firm against the devil's schemes, reminding us that our battles are not against flesh and blood but against spiritual forces of evil.

The development of **Discernment as a Gift and Skill** is crucial. This dual aspect of discernment, as both a spiritual gift and a practical skill, underscores the need for continuous growth in our ability to distinguish truth from deception. Regular prayer, engagement with the Holy Scriptures, and reflective community interactions enhance our discernment, enabling us to perceive subtleties that might otherwise go unnoticed.

Implementing **Protective Strategies** involves both spiritual practices and practical steps to safeguard ourselves and our communities. Regular educational sessions on the nature of deceit, coupled with fostering environments of open communication and accountability, serve as bulwarks against the inroads of deception.

The **Role of Community** in providing support and accountability cannot be overstated. A strong, vigilant community acts as a crucial check against the spread of deceit, providing a network of support that bolsters each member's ability to stand firm against manipulation and betrayal.

Ignoring signs of deceit can lead to severe consequences, as outlined in the point on **Consequences of Unaddressed Deception**. When deceit goes unchecked, it can erode the very foundations of trust and integrity upon which healthy relationships and societies are built.

Finally, **Empowerment Through Truth** is our greatest defense. Embracing truth and promoting transparency in all our dealings ensures a life of integrity. Truth not only protects but also liberates, providing a clear path in a world rife with confusion and deceit.

As we forge ahead, armed with knowledge and fortified by divine wisdom, let us commit to a vigilant and proactive stance against the treachery and trickery that seek to undermine our faith and communal life.

**REFLECTIVE QUESTIONS**

1. Can you recall a time when you faced deception in a close relationship? How did you handle it, and what did you learn from the experience?
2. How do you cultivate discernment in your daily life? What spiritual disciplines support you in this endeavor?
3. Reflect on a situation where community support helped you avoid a deceitful situation. What role did community play in your discernment process?
4. Consider a time when ignoring signs of deceit had consequences in your life. What signs did you overlook, and why?
5. How can you use your experiences with deceit to help others in your community strengthen their ability to discern truth from lies?

**ACTIONABLE STEPS**

- **Cultivate a Daily Discipline of Truth**: Engage daily with the Scriptures and prayer to build a foundation of truth that guards against deception.
- **Equip Yourself and Others**: Provide or attend workshops on discernment and understanding biblical teachings on truth and deception to strengthen yourself and your community.
- **Engage in Open Conversations**: Create safe spaces in your community where experiences of deceit can be shared and discussed openly, enhancing collective vigilance and support.

. . .

**JOURNALING Prompt**

Reflect on your personal vulnerabilities to treachery and trickery. What specific situations or types of relationships make you most susceptible to deception? How can you apply the insights from this chapter to fortify yourself against such vulnerabilities?

# CHAPTER 14

# TURN THE STORM: END-TIME PERIL, END-TIME GLORY

**Stand firm and behold the restoration of God's glory. Let His spirit infuse your every endeavor with divine power and wisdom as you navigate the complexities of these times. 1 Corinthians 9:24**

**"Do you not know that those who run in a race all run, but one receives the prize? Run in such a way that you may obtain it."**

In these challenging yet transformative times, it's crucial to recognize the dual nature of the period we're living through—the **End-Times Glory and Peril**. This era is marked by significant challenges but also by unprecedented opportunities for God's glory to manifest in powerful ways. The biblical prophet Elijah, a man like us, endured periods of wilderness and isolation that prepared him for monumental tasks. Similarly, God is molding us through our trials, equipping us to

**reflect His glory** and act as catalysts for change in this pivotal era.

As we journey through these times, it's essential to understand the significance of our **covenantal alignment with God**. Just as ancient covenants required steadfastness and faithfulness, our spiritual covenant with God necessitates a commitment to His statutes and a life lived in harmony with His divine will. This alignment is not merely about adhering to rules; it's about positioning ourselves to fully experience and radiate God's glory, which moves according to His plans and purposes.

Navigating through life's challenges requires the wisdom to know when we can alter circumstances and when to align with the divine flow. Not all storms can be averted, but through prayer and spiritual insight, they can often be turned. The concept of **Turning the Storms** is pivotal in understanding how we can influence both our environment and the spiritual realm. By invoking God's power through focused prayer, we can shift the atmosphere around us, creating outcomes that reflect His glory and purposes.

The anointing reminiscent of Elijah, which I refer to as the **Spirit and Power of Elijah**, is particularly relevant today. This anointing is about turning hearts back to God, realigning the wayward with divine intention, and restoring broken relationships through repentance and reconciliation. It's an anointing that also involves **repentance and a return to God's ways**, echoing the call for teshuvah—turning back to God with our whole heart.

In this context, **the role of glory in the End Times** is transformative. The glory of God doesn't just sit passively; it moves dynamically across the earth, sparking revival, awakening, and reformation. As believers, we're called to discern these movements of the Holy Spirit and respond by positioning ourselves as conduits of His power and grace. This requires a deep understanding of the **movements of God's glory**, recognizing when to push forward and when to yield, allowing His spirit to lead the way.

Understanding the **interplay of natural and spiritual storms** gives us insight into the broader workings of God's kingdom on earth. The battles we face are not just physical but are deeply entrenched in the spiritual fabric of our reality. By standing in the gap through **prayer and intercession**, we engage in spiritual warfare that has tangible effects in the natural world.

The **Turnaround Anointing** brings to light the power of divine judgment in favor of the saints. It's a reminder that despite the enemy's attempts to thwart God's plans, His decrees will ultimately establish justice and set the stage for His kingdom's expansion on earth. This involves not only personal deliverance but also **deliverance and restoration** for communities and nations.

Amidst these profound truths, we must also focus on practical engagement. The prophetic and revolutionary aspects of God's move in this era call for active participation. **Revolution and Realignment** involve embracing the changes God is instigating in the church, society, and our personal lives, aligning ourselves with His purposes to see His kingdom come on earth as it is in heaven.

Finally, I invite you to consider your role in this divine narrative. What does it mean for you to prepare for and participate in God's unfolding plan? How can you live out the call to **prepare the way for Christ's coming**? Engage deeply with these thoughts as you reflect on your personal journey with God and your part in His grand design.

May this understanding not only enlighten you but also ignite a passion within you to pursue God's heart and His purposes for your life and your community.

. . .

**REFLECTIVE QUESTIONS**

1. How does understanding the dual nature of End-Time Peril and Glory change your perspective on current global events?
2. In what ways can you align more closely with God's covenant and reflect His glory in your daily life?
3. What practical steps can you take to turn the storms in your life or community through prayer and action?
4. How does the concept of the Spirit and Power of Elijah resonate with your personal spiritual journey?
5. What role do you see yourself playing in the prophetic and revolutionary changes God is initiating in this era?

**ACTIONABLE STEPS**

1. **Cultivate** a deeper relationship with God by setting aside regular times for prayer and meditation on His Word, focusing on what it means to live in covenant with Him.
2. **Equip** yourself with knowledge of the Holy Scriptures and the history of God's movements on earth, which can guide your understanding of the current times.
3. **Engage** in your community or church with initiatives that reflect the turning of hearts back to God, whether through outreach, teaching, or intercessory prayer.

. . .

**JOURNALING Prompt**

Reflect on a recent challenge or storm in your life. How did you see God moving in that situation? Write about how you can apply the principles of turning storms and embracing God's glory to future challenges.

# D DESTINY IMAGE

Destiny Image is a prophetic Christian publisher dedicated to empowering believers through Spirit-led messages. Our mission is to equip and inspire individuals to fulfill their God-given destinies by providing transformative resources that resonate with the Charismatic and Pentecostal faith.

We specialize in books, blogs, and back cover copies that reflect prophetic insights, dynamic teachings, and testimonies of faith. Our commitment to fostering spiritual growth and kingdom impact makes Destiny Image a beacon for those seeking to deepen their relationship with God and embrace their calling in the power of the Holy Spirit.